THE STORY OF HOW PETER BECA

FINDING
NEVERLAND
A NEW BROADWAY MUSICAL

HAL•LEONARD®
CORPORATION

7777 W. BLUEMOUND RD. P.O. BOX 13819 MILWAUKEE, WI 53213

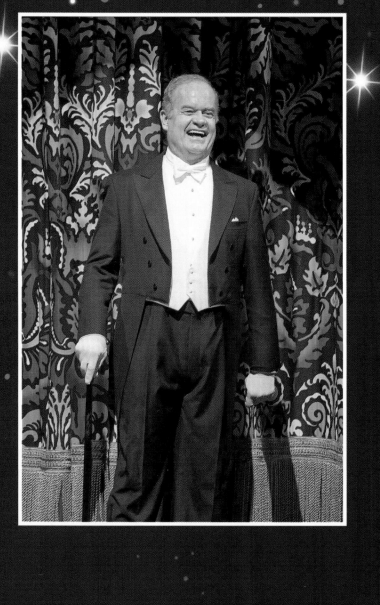

PRESENT

FINDING NEVERLAND

BOOK BY
JAMES GRAHAM

MUSIC & LYRICS BY
GARY BARLOW & ELIOT KENNEDY

Based on the Miramax Motion Picture written by David Magee
and the play The Man Who Was Peter Pan by Allan Knee

SCENIC DESIGN	COSTUME DESIGN	LIGHTING DESIGN	SOUND DESIGN	PROJECTION DESIGN
SCOTT PASK	SUTTIRAT ANNE LARLARB	KENNETH POSNER	JONATHAN DEANS	JON DRISCOLL

MUSIC DIRECTOR
MARY-MITCHELL CAMPBELL

VOCAL DESIGNER
ANNMARIE MILAZZO

EXECUTIVE PRODUCER
NATIONAL ARTISTS MANAGEMENT COMPANY
BARRY & FRAN WEISSIER
ALECIA PARKER

EXECUTIVE PRODUCER
WEINSTEIN LIVE ENTERTAINMENT
VICTORIA PARKER

GENERAL MANAGER
B.J. HOLT

PRODUCED BY
HARVEY WEINSTEIN

ORCHESTRATIONS BY
SIMON HALE

MUSICAL SUPERVISION AND
DANCE AND INCIDENTAL MUSIC ARRANGEMENTS BY
DAVID CHASE

CHOREOGRAPHY BY
MIA MICHAELS

DIRECTED BY
DIANE PAULUS

ISBN 978-1-4950-5675-8

7777 W. BLUEMOUND RD. P.O. BOX 13819 MILWAUKEE, WI 53213

Visit Hal Leonard Online at
www.halleonard.com

What a dream it has been to be able to write music for this wonderful story.

In addition to that the chance to work again with my friend Eliot Kennedy.

We've laughed, cried and cheered our way through this whole experience.

Its been challenging and relentless but truly inspirational.

I hope this is a door opening to a whole new part of my musical journey.

Gary Barlow (June 2015)

PROLOGUE

Words and Music by ELIOT KENNEDY
and GARY BARLOW

IF THE WORLD TURNED UPSIDE DOWN

Words and Music by ELIOT KENNEDY
and GARY BARLOW

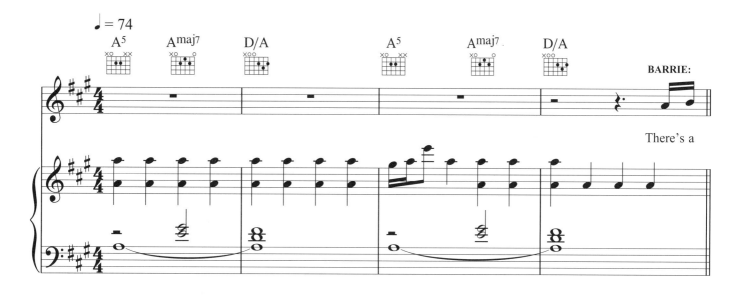

BARRIE:

There's a

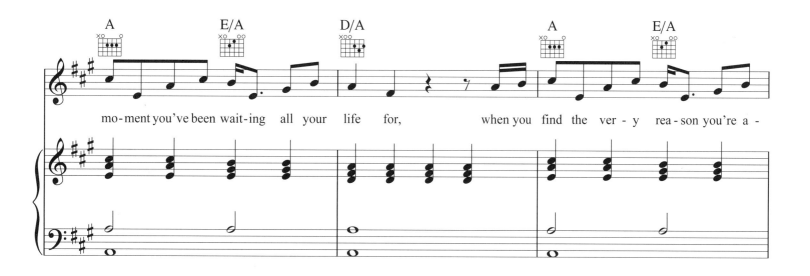

mo-ment you've been wait-ing all your life for, when you find the ver-y rea-son you're a-

-live for. And it hap-pens when you seem to least ex-pect it, all at

ALL OF LONDON IS HERE TONIGHT

Words and Music by ELIOT KENNEDY
and GARY BARLOW

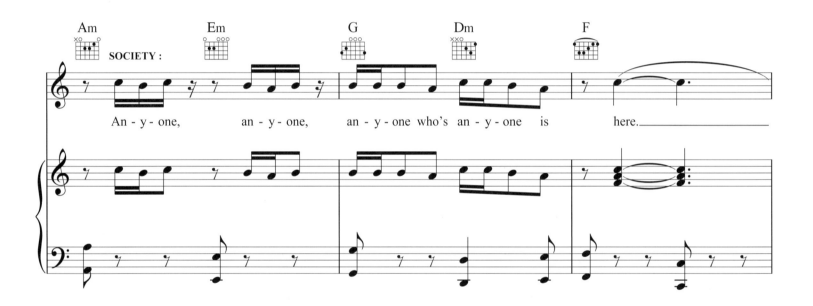

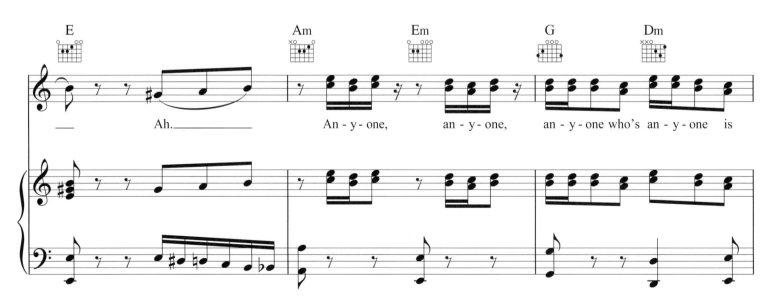

here.   FROHMAN:
                                                            From

Lon-don's West End   to the Great White Way   I've dis-cov-ered the best play-wrights

work-ing to-day.   You were "Wilde" a-bout Os-car, so I gave you more, I sup-

-por-ted Ber-nard___ when no one was "Shaw".

24

THE PIRATES OF KENSINGTON

Words and Music by ELIOT KENNEDY
and GARY BARLOW

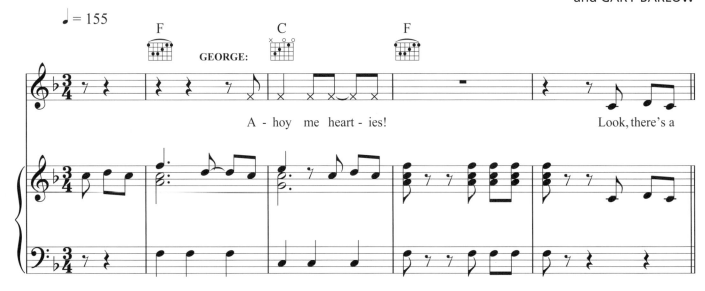

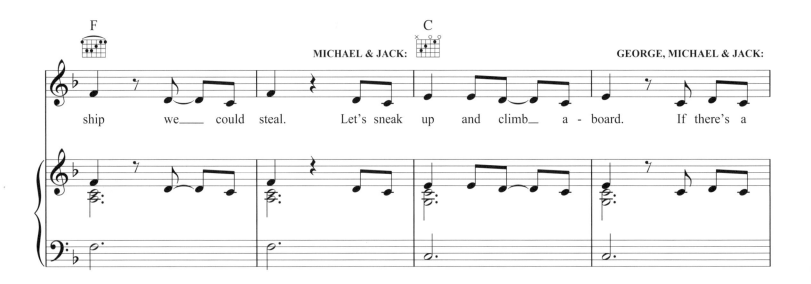

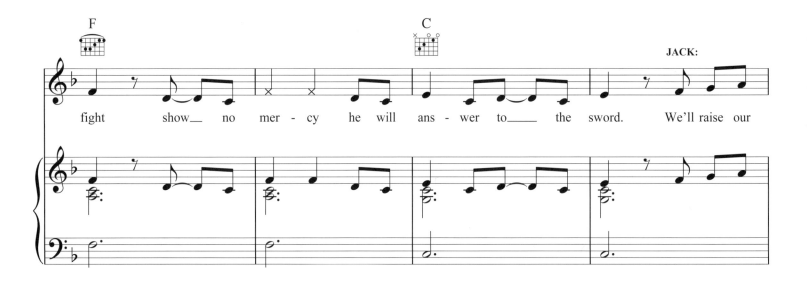

BELIEVE

Words and Music by ELIOT KENNEDY
and GARY BARLOW

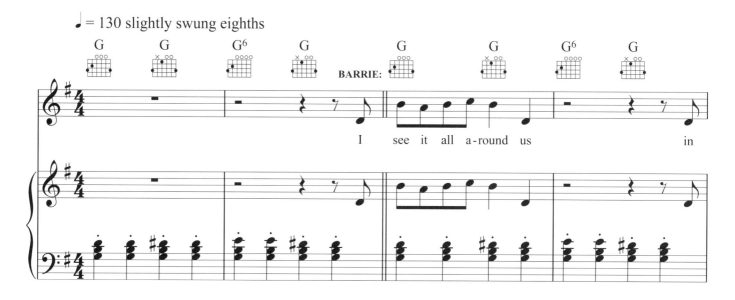

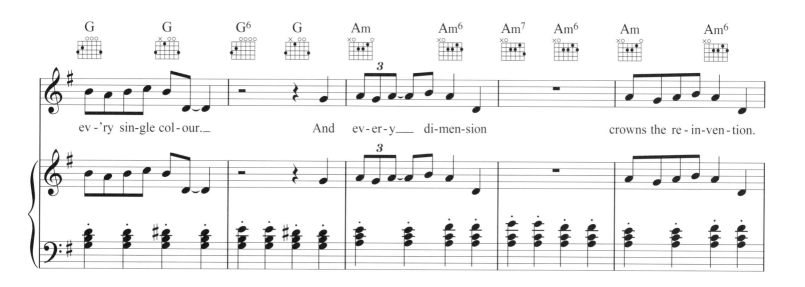

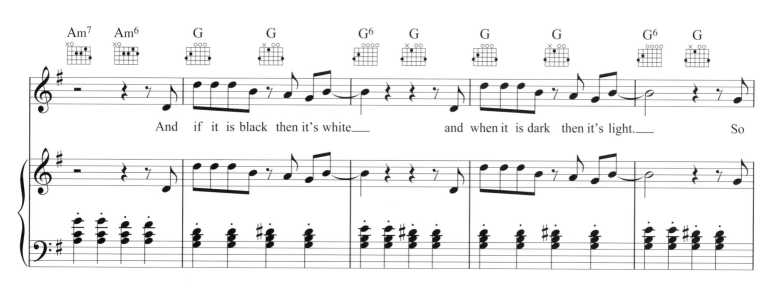

WE OWN THE NIGHT

Words and Music by ELIOT KENNEDY
and GARY BARLOW

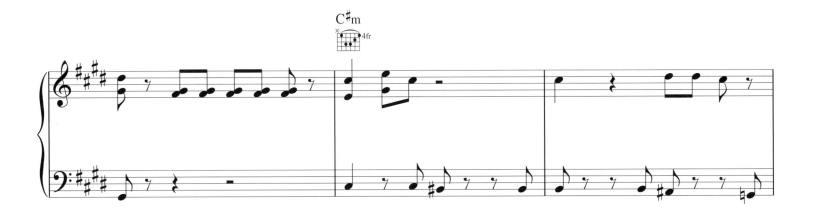

G♯
4fr
ALL:
Oh how we
D♭
4fr
F
love this mad - ness, so en - ter - tain - ing, we'll be shar - ing glad - ness,
G♭
they'll be com - plain - ing. We'll be right un - der their no - ses but we're
D♭
4fr
F
just out of sight. I'm sure there'll be a price to pay (I'm

SYLVIA'S LULLABY

Words and Music by ELIOT KENNEDY
and GARY BARLOW

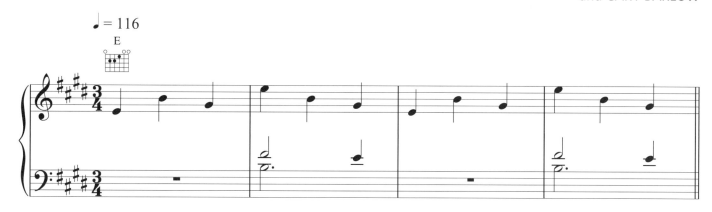

SYLVIA:

Qui - et - ly, hush now to sleep, on the

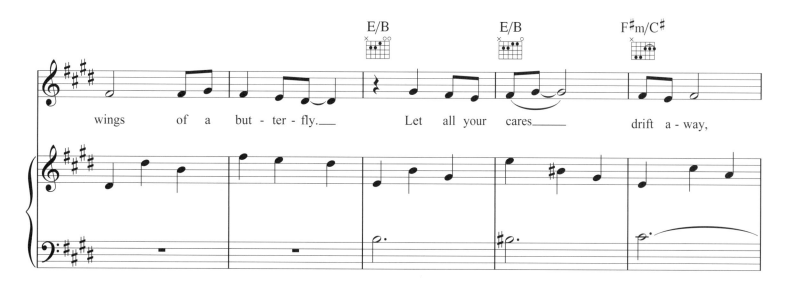

wings of a but - ter - fly. Let all your cares drift a - way,

ALL THAT MATTERS

Words and Music by ELIOT KENNEDY
and GARY BARLOW

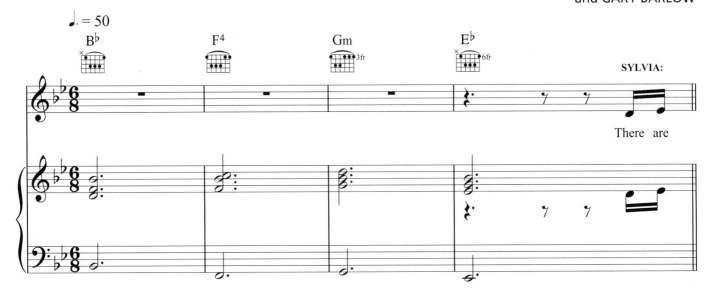

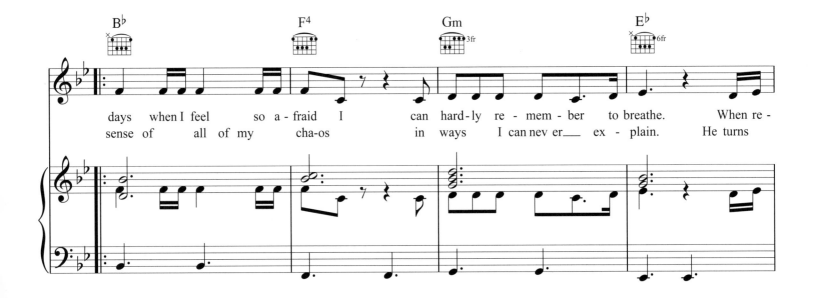

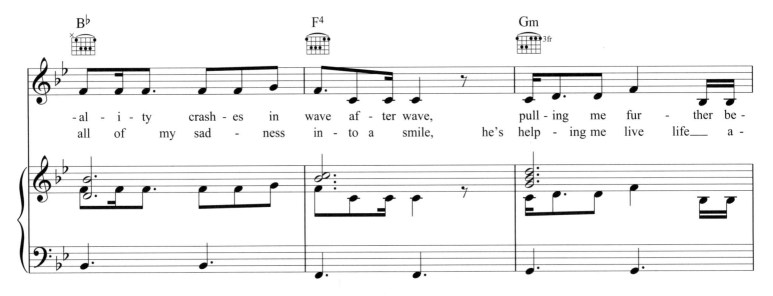

NEVERLAND

Words and Music by ELIOT KENNEDY
and GARY BARLOW

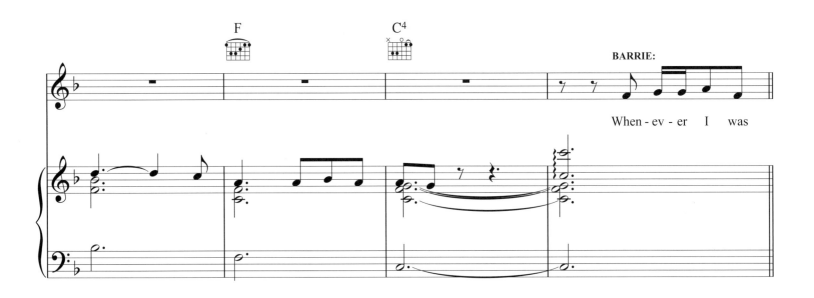

When - ev - er I was

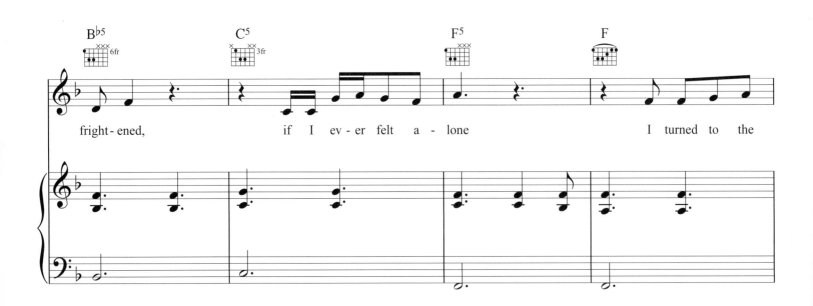

fright - ened,   if I ev - er felt a - lone   I turned to the

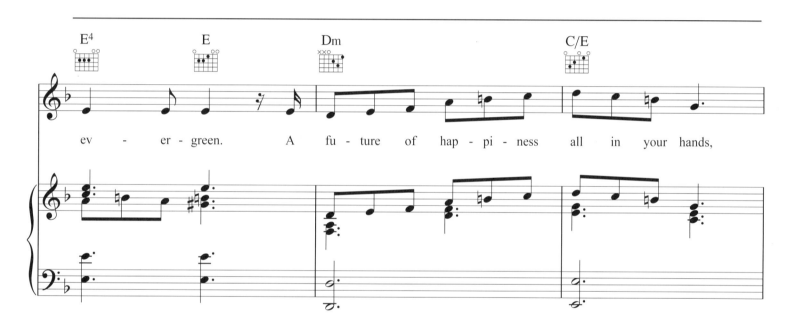

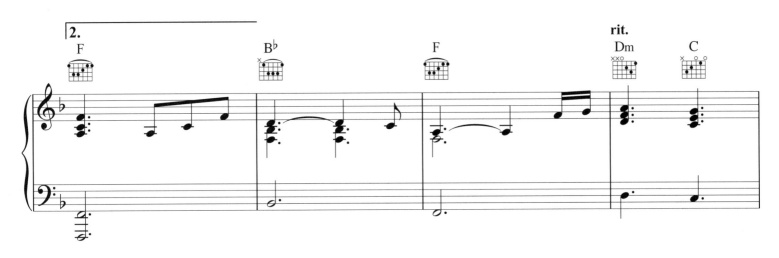

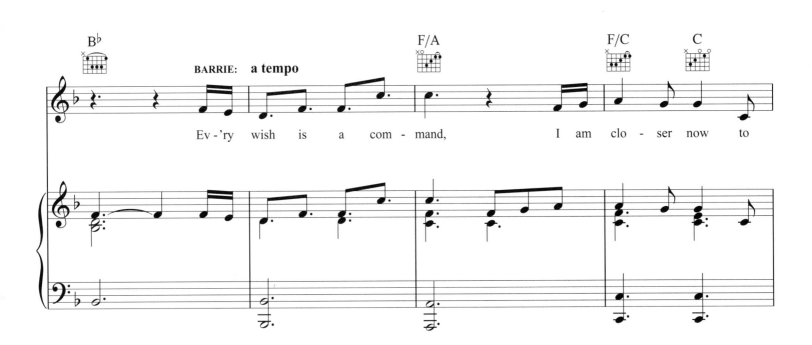

Ev -'ry wish is a com - mand, I am clo - ser now to

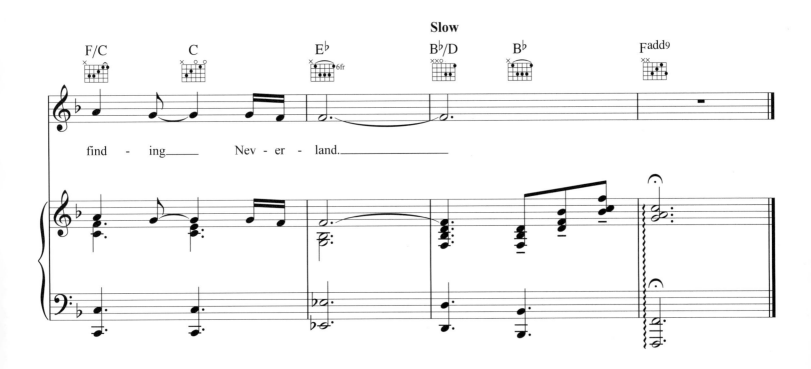

find - ing____ Nev - er - land._____

CIRCUS OF YOUR MIND

Words and Music by ELIOT KENNEDY
and GARY BARLOW

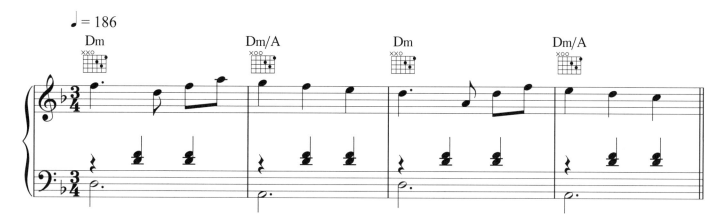

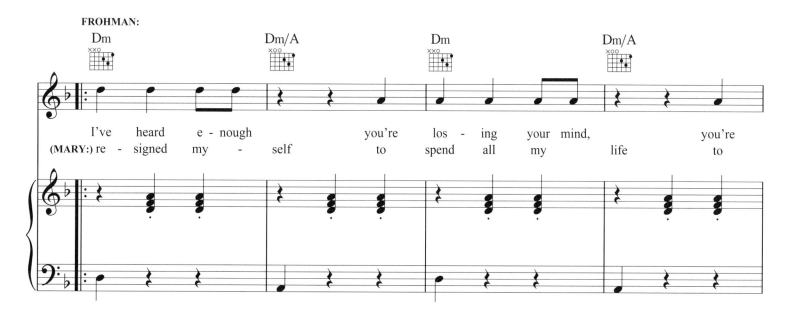

FROHMAN:

I've heard e - nough you're los - ing your mind, you're
(MARY:) re - signed my - self to spend all my life

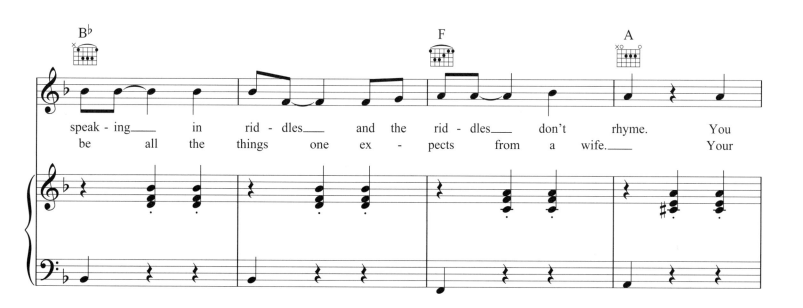

speak - ing in rid - dles and the rid - dles don't rhyme. You
be all the things one ex - pects from a wife. Your

(Spare us your cro-co-dile tears, Mis-ter Bar-rie.)

(Tick tock tick tock

tick tock tick tock.)

♩ = 170

66

LIVE BY THE HOOK

Words and Music by ELIOT KENNEDY
and GARY BARLOW

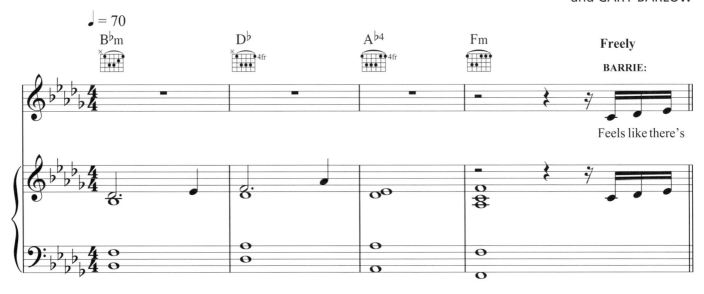

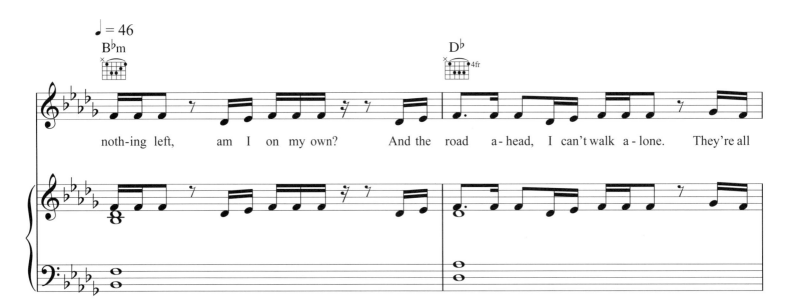

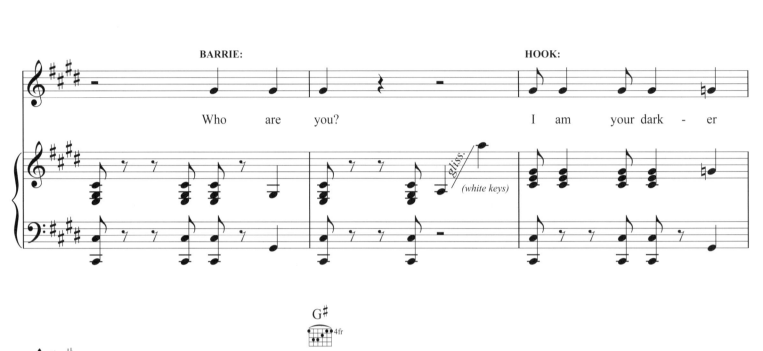

BARRIE:

HOOK:

Who are you?

I am your dark - er

side, the one you keep in shad - ows, pre - fer to hide.

Deep in your heart you can't de - ny all of your fears keep

STRONGER

Words and Music by ELIOT KENNEDY
and GARY BARLOW

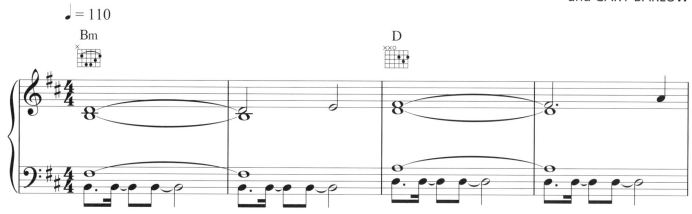

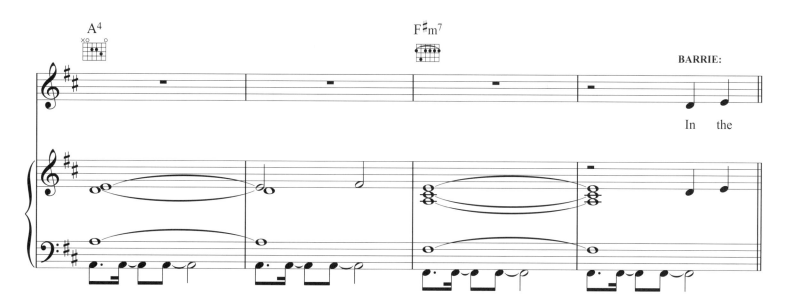

BARRIE:

BARRIE, HOOK & PIRATES:

THE WORLD IS UPSIDE DOWN

Words and Music by ELIOT KENNEDY
and GARY BARLOW

Wel-come my friends,_ glad you could join me on this most aus - pi-cious day._

_ I hope you'll for-give_ mis takes and er-rors, we're just

WHAT YOU MEAN TO ME

Words and Music by ELIOT KENNEDY
and GARY BARLOW

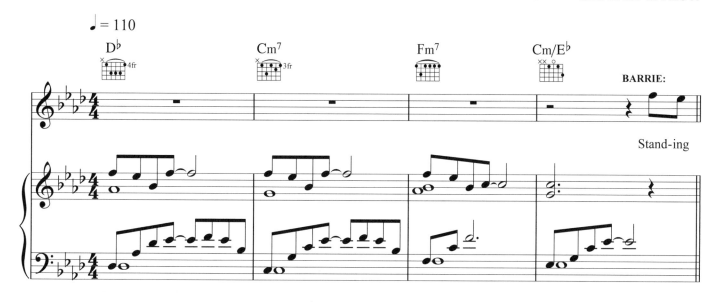

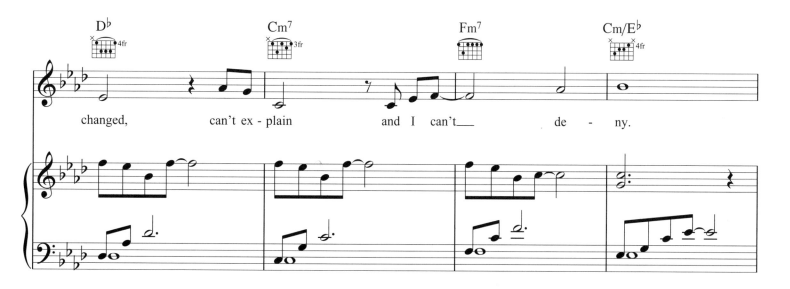

PLAY

Words and Music by ELIOT KENNEDY
and GARY BARLOW

WE'RE ALL MADE OF STARS

Words and Music by ELIOT KENNEDY
and GARY BARLOW

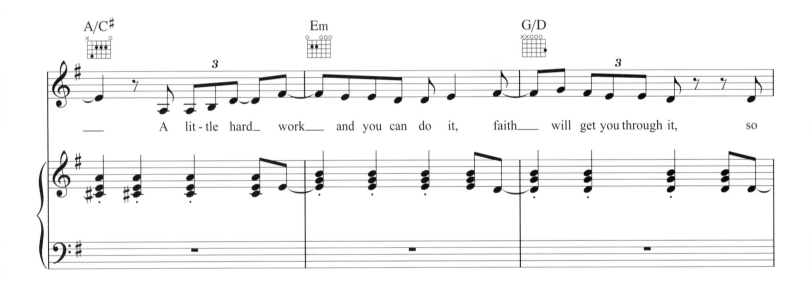

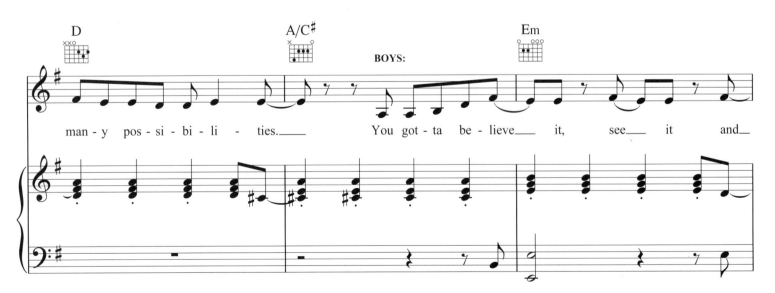

WHEN YOUR FEET DON'T TOUCH THE GROUND

Words and Music by ELIOT KENNEDY
and GARY BARLOW

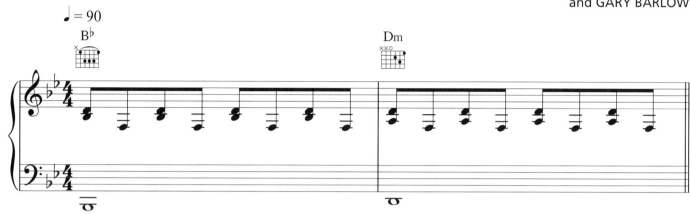

BARRIE: When did life be-come so com-pli-ca-ted? Years of too much thought and
PETER: Ev-'ry day just feels a lit-tle long-er. Why am I the on-ly one not

time I wast-ed. And in each line up-on my face is
get-ting strong-er? Run-ning 'round pre-tend-ing life's a play, it

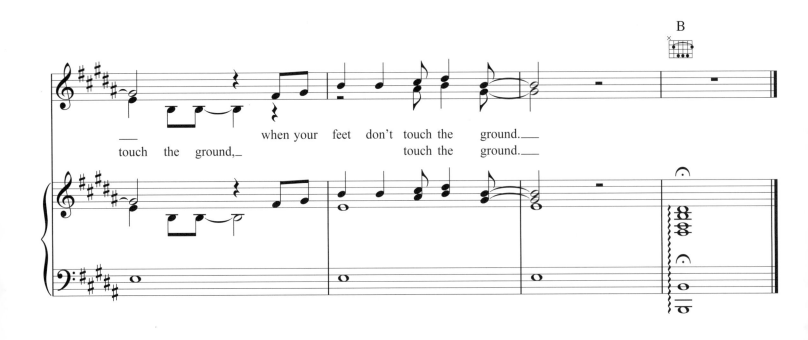

SOMETHING ABOUT THIS NIGHT

Words and Music by ELIOT KENNEDY
and GARY BARLOW

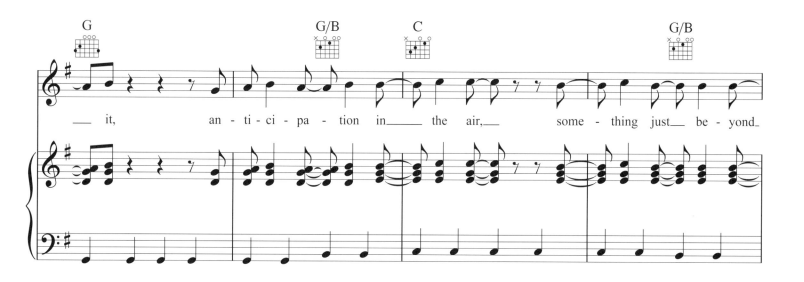

NEVERLAND
(Reprise)

Words and Music by ELIOT KENNEDY
and GARY BARLOW

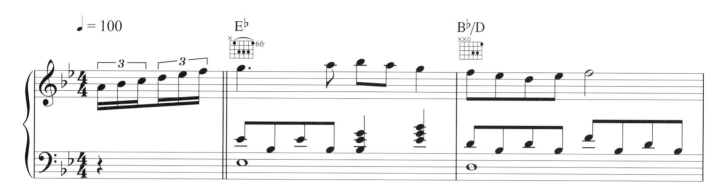

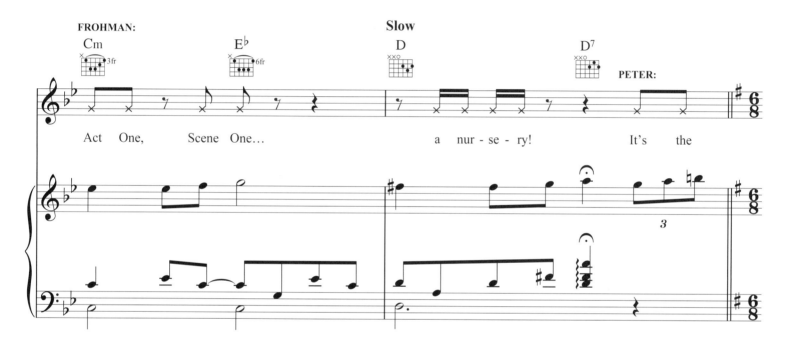

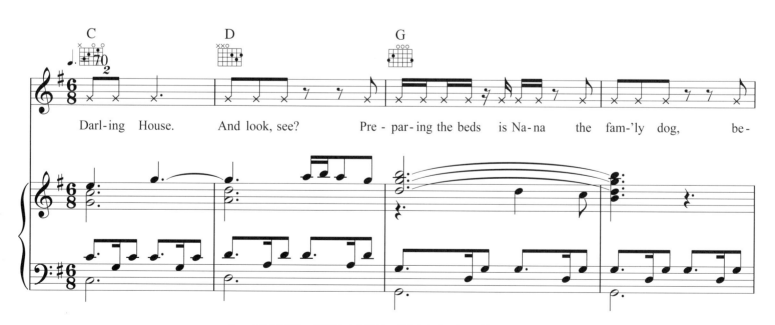

PETER: clev- er! And then, this is my fav-'rite bit. Pe- ter shows Wen-dy how to fly! We can

BARRIE:

sail a- way to- night on a sea of pure moon- light. We can

na- vi- gate the stars to bring us back home._____ In a

place so far a- way. We are young, that's how we'll

BOYS:

133

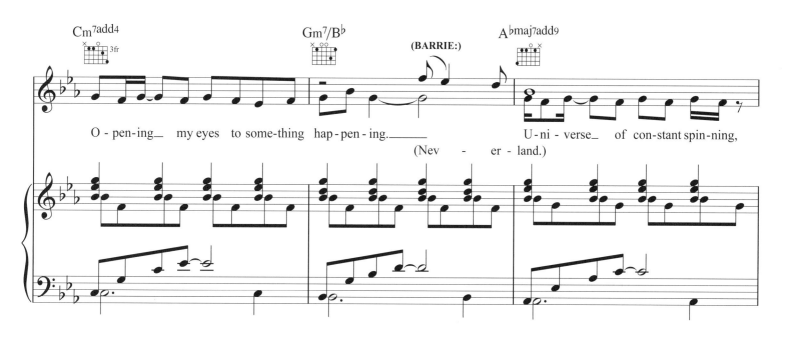

G
D/F#
SYLVIA:
Bm7
MICHAEL:
drank his med-i-cine be-cause it was poi-soned. She drank it to save his life? Is... is Tink dy-ing?
GEORGE:
A/C#
Fmaj7
C/E
PETER:
Look. Her light is grow ing faint. If it goes out, that means she's dead. She says
Am
Em/B
Fmaj7
BARRIE:
she thinks she could get well a-gain, if child-ren be-lieve in fai-ries. And do you? Do
C/E
Slow
Am
G/B
PETER:
MRS DuMAURIER:
BARRIE:
you be-lieve in fai-ries? If you be-lieve, clap your hands! I be-lieve! Come a-long, child-ren! Ev-'ry-one!

FINALE

Words and Music by ELIOT KENNEDY
and GARY BARLOW

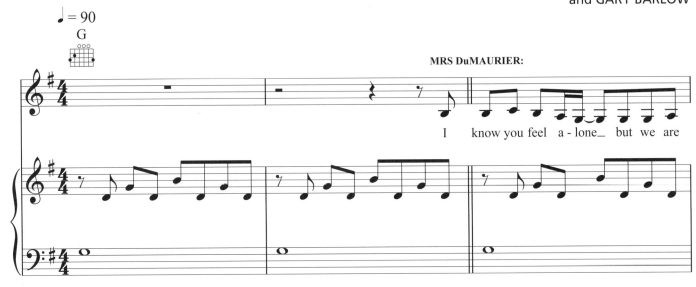

MRS DuMAURIER:

I know you feel a-lone_ but we are

here   be - side you.   She left the stars up in the sky so they   could guide   you.

And you will see her___ in your dreams,   for Nev-er-land___ is clo-ser___ than it

PLAY
(Ensemble Version)

Words and Music by ELIOT KENNEDY
and GARY BARLOW

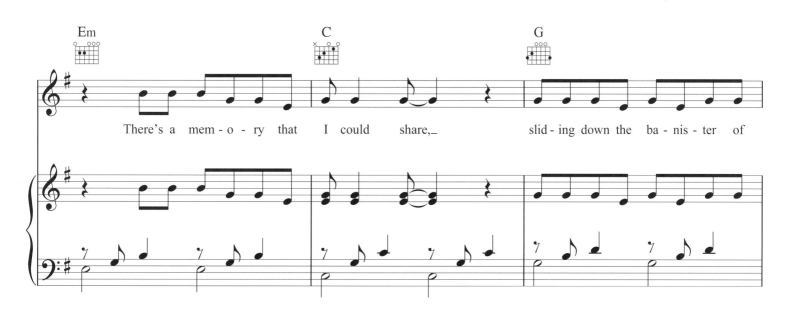

There's a mem-o-ry that I could share,___ slid-ing down the ba-nis-ter of

our old stairs.___ On-ly for a mo-ment___ in mid-air,___

fly._____ I used to dream I was a

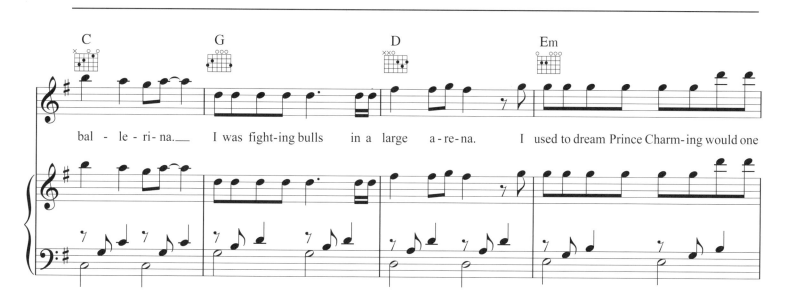

bal - le - ri - na.___ I was fight-ing bulls in a large a - re - na. I used to dream Prince Charm-ing would one

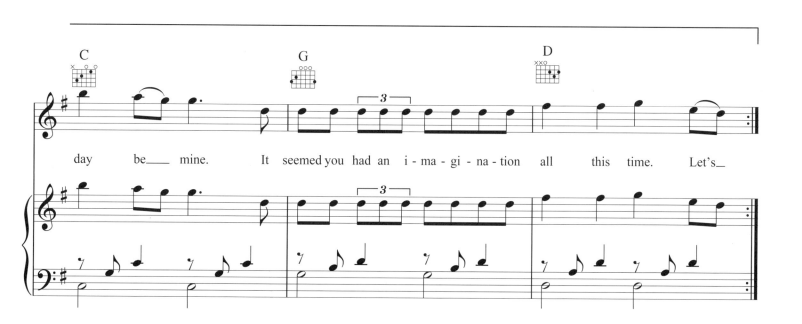

day be___ mine. It seemed you had an i - ma - gi - na - tion all this time. Let's___